Bees

ABDO
Publishing Company

Big Buddy BOOKS
Insects

Julie Murray

VISIT US AT
www.abdopublishing.com

Published by ABDO Publishing Company, 8000 West 78th Street, Edina, Minnesota 55439.

Copyright © 2011 by Abdo Consulting Group, Inc. International copyrights reserved in all countries. No part of this book may be reproduced in any form without written permission from the publisher. Big Buddy Books™ is a trademark and logo of ABDO Publishing Company.

Printed in the United States of America, North Mankato, Minnesota.
042010
092010

 PRINTED ON RECYCLED PAPER

Coordinating Series Editor: Rochelle Baltzer
Editor: Sarah Tieck
Contributing Editors: Heidi M.D. Elston, Megan M. Gunderson, BreAnn Rumsch, Marcia Zappa
Graphic Design: Maria Hosley
Cover Photograph: *Image Ideas Inc.*
Interior Photographs/Illustrations: *Image Ideas Inc.* (p. 9); *iStockphoto*: ©iStockphoto.com/Antagain (p. 7), ©iStockphoto.com/vtupinamba (p. 5); *John Foxx Images* (pp. 22, 30); *Peter Arnold, Inc.*: ©Biosphoto (p. 13), ©Biosphoto/Thiriet Claudius (p. 21), ©Biosphoto/Delobelle Jean-Philippe (p. 14), Hans Pfletschinger (p. 11), WILDLIFE (pp. 17, 26, 27); *Photo Researchers, Inc.*: Scott Camazine (p. 9), Crown Copyright courtesy of Central Science Laboratory (p. 25), Valerie Giles (p. 15); *Shutterstock*: abxyz (p. 9); Mircea BEZERGHEANU (p. 25), Dainis Derics (p. 23), Liga Lauzuma (p. 19), Steve Lovegrove (p. 23), roseburn (p. 22), Adam Tinney (p. 30), Juehua Yin (p. 25), Joanna Zopoth-Lipiejko (p. 11), ZTS (p. 29).

Library of Congress Cataloging-in-Publication Data

Murray, Julie, 1969-
 Bees / Julie Murray.
   p. cm. -- (Insects)
 ISBN 978-1-61613-482-2
 1. Bees--Juvenile literature. I. Title. II. Series: Murray, Julie, 1969- Insects.
 QL565.2.M87 2011
 595.79'9--dc22
                    2010000786

Contents

Insect World

Millions of insects live throughout the world. They are found on the ground, in the air, and in the water. Some have existed since before there were dinosaurs!

Bees are one type of insect. They live in many different places, including jungles, woods, and fields. You may even find bees in a city or in your backyard!

Bug Bite!

Bees are closely related to sawflies, wasps, and ants.

Many bees have hairy bodies!

A Bee's Body

Like all insects, a bee has three main body parts. These are the head, the **thorax**, and the **abdomen**.

A bee's head has five eyes, two antennae, and a special tongue. The antennae help the bee smell. The tongue is called a proboscis (pruh-BAH-suhs). Bees use it like a straw to suck nectar from flowers.

A bee's six legs and four wings connect to its thorax. Many bees have pollen baskets on their back legs. The bee's abdomen holds important **organs**.

Bug Bite! The smallest bees are less than .1 inches (.25 cm) long. The largest measure about 1.5 inches (4 cm).

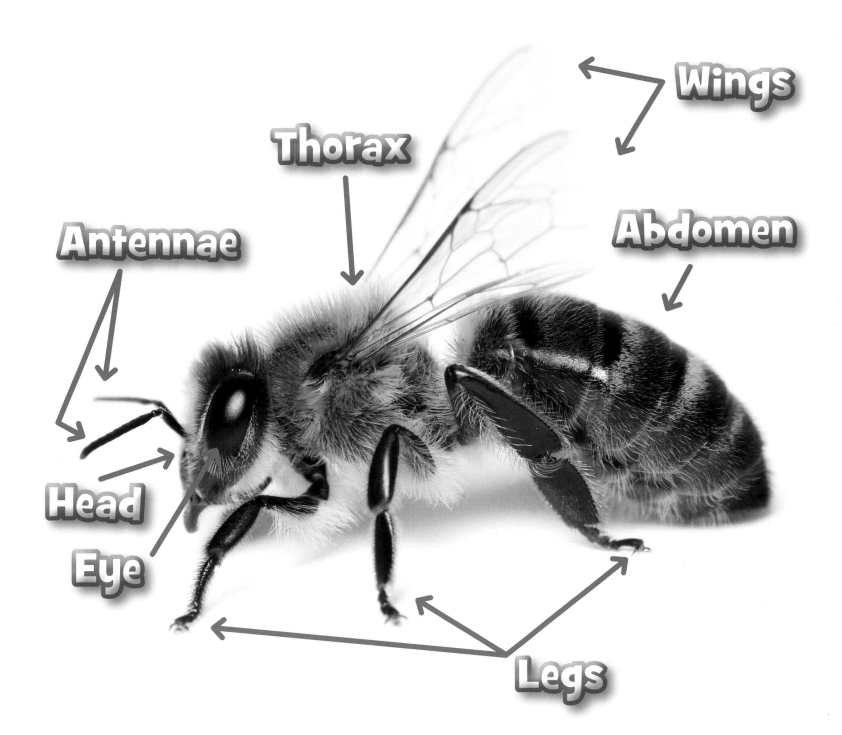

Wings

Thorax

Antennae

Abdomen

Head

Eye

Legs

A Bee's Life

There are many types of bees. Most bees live alone and care for themselves. They are called solitary bees.

Bees that live in colonies are called social bees. These bees build a nest to share. And, they work together to feed and **protect** their colony's young.

Carpenter bees are solitary bees.

Bumblebees *(left)* and honeybees *(below)* are both social bees.

Bug Bite!

There are more than 20,000 kinds of bees! Of those, about 500 are social bees.

9

Life Begins

A bee goes through four different life stages. These stages are egg, larva, pupa, and adult.

All bees begin life as an egg. Honeybees lay eggs in honeycomb cells. Other types of bees lay eggs in different kinds of nests.

Bug Bite!

A honeycomb has wax cells with six-sided walls. Honeybees store honey, pollen, and eggs in the cells.

Life Cycle of a Bumblebee

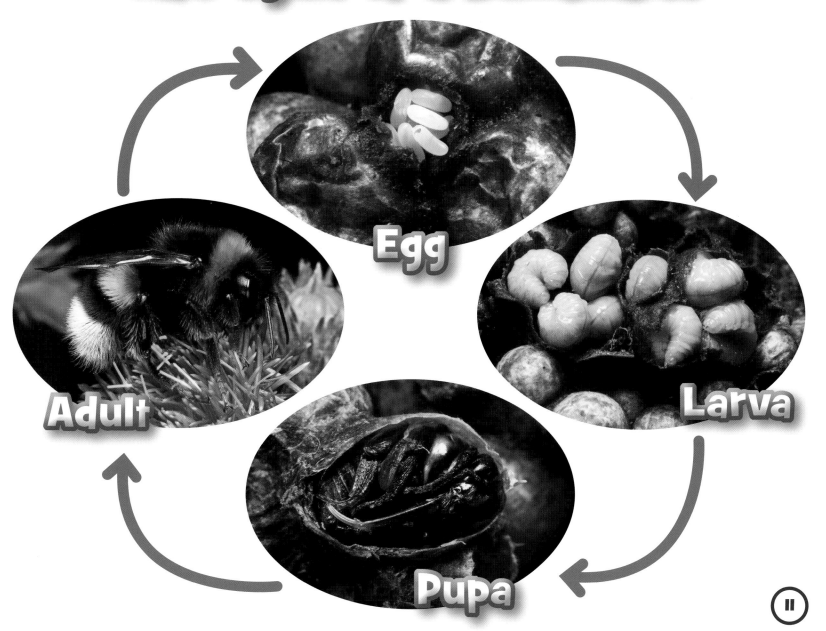

Egg

Larva

Pupa

Adult

11

In the egg, a wormlike larva forms. Then, the larva **hatches** from the egg. It has no legs or wings.

Adult honeybees feed larvae a special food called royal jelly. Other types of bee larvae eat beebread left by their mothers. Beebread is a mix of pollen and nectar or honey.

When the larva has grown enough, it spins a cocoon. A pupa forms inside the cocoon. Later, an adult bee crawls out.

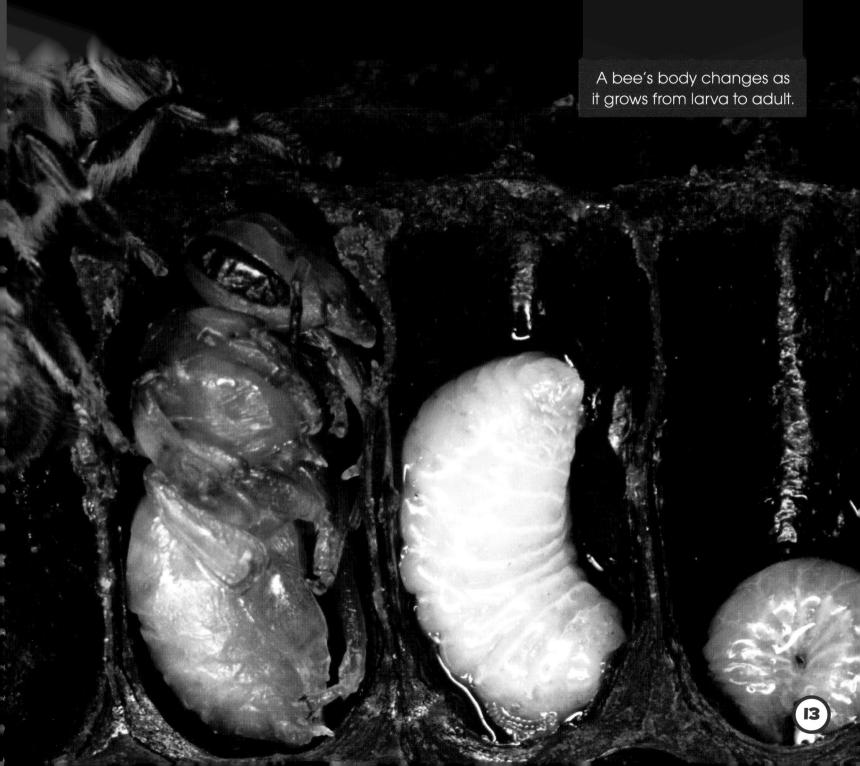

A bee's body changes as it grows from larva to adult.

Carpenter bees tunnel through wood to build their nests.

Bug Bite!

Some bees use their bodies like a ruler to make their homes fit them.

Small Family

Solitary bees live and work alone. Carpenter bees are one type of solitary bee. They make homes by cutting into wood with their sharp jaws.

When they hatch, carpenter bee larvae take care of themselves.

Adult carpenter bees rest in nests during winter. In spring, they **mate**. Then, females build nests for their eggs. Both parents die before their eggs **hatch**.

The Queen Bee

Social bees live in colonies. Different species live differently. But most colonies have one queen, many female workers, and a few male drones.

Honeybees are a type of social bee. The honeybee queen is the colony's leader. She lives one to five years. During her life, the queen mates with different drones. A single queen may lay thousands of eggs.

Queen

Drone

Worker

A bee's body is suited to its job in the colony. For example, a queen is large to help her lay many eggs.

Worker Bees

Most social bees are female worker bees. Worker bees do important jobs in the colony. Some help build the nest. Others care for the queen and her young. Still other workers collect food. Many worker bees change jobs as they grow.

Worker bees look for warm flowers. Drinking warm nectar helps their bodies stay warm.

Drones

A small amount of social bees are male. Male bees are called drones. Usually, drones do not collect food, build nests, or care for young. Their only job is to **mate**.

Bumblebees are one type of social bee. Male bumblebees live just long enough to mate. This makes sure bumblebee **species** survive.

Bug Bite!

When a bee flaps its wings, it makes a buzzing sound. Different species make different sounds.

Honeybee drones have extra large eyes. This helps them see the queen.

Honey

A bee flies from flower to flower. Its wings allow it to travel a couple of miles at a time!

A bee can carry about half its weight in nectar and still fly! Can you spot the pollen basket on its leg?

It takes nectar from about 2 million flowers to make just one pound (.5 kg) of honey.

Honeybees make honey in their hives. They eat honey and feed it to their young. This food supply helps them survive winter.

To make honey, a bee first drinks nectar from flowers. It uses its proboscis to suck up the sweet liquid. The nectar is broken down in a special **organ** called the honey stomach. Then, the bee spits up the nectar. It is stored in a honeycomb cell. There, it turns into honey.

Danger Zone

Bees face many predators. These include dragonflies, birds, and tiny bugs called mites.

When predators see bright yellow and black bees, most stay away. Usually, such colors mean poison or danger.

Wasps are a bee enemy. They steal honey from hives.

Bee-eater birds eat many kinds of flying insects, including bees.

Varroa mites attack honeybee larvae and adults. They can spread from one hive to another.

Bug Bite!

Some honeybees use heat to protect themselves from wasps. They gather in a group around a wasp. They move their bodies very fast. The heat they make is strong enough to kill the wasp.

Bug Bite!

Some bees are stingless. Female stingless bees have small stingers, but they don't use them.

Male bees do not have stingers.

When predators do not stay away, bees **protect** themselves. To do this, they often use their stingers. Most bees can sting repeatedly with their smooth stingers.

A female bee's stinger is part of her abdomen. It lets out a type of poison, or venom.

Many worker honeybees have a different type of stinger. It has **barbs** on the end. So, it may get stuck when they sting. Losing a stinger kills a bee. But a bee will give up its life to **protect** its hive and queen.

Special Insects

Bees do important work in the natural world. They carry pollen from one flower to another. Plants need this movement of pollen to live and grow. And humans and animals depend on plants for food. In this way, bees support the world's food supply.

Some bee **species** are in danger of dying out. Scientists are working to save them. This helps **protect** life on Earth.

Bug Bite!

Some bee sting venom is being used to help people who have pain in their joints.

Bees carry pollen to fruit and vegetable plants. Oranges, tomatoes, and squash need bees to grow.

Bug-O-Rama

How hard do worker bees really work?

Most worker bees start work as soon as they become adults. When honeybee workers come out of their cocoons, they clean their cells. This gets each cell ready for its next egg.

How do honeybees talk to each other?

Honeybees use movements to tell each other where to find food. They do special dances. Honeybees may run, circle, and shake.

Are bees dangerous to people?

Some people are allergic to bees. If they get stung, they can become very sick. But usually bees do not sting unless they are bothered. So if you see a bee, you should leave it alone.

Important Words

abdomen (AB-duh-muhn) the back part of an insect's body.

barb a sharp point that sticks out backward and prevents easy removal.

hatch to be born from an egg.

jaws a mouthpart that allows for holding, crushing, and chewing.

mate to join as a couple in order to reproduce, or have babies.

organ a body part that does a special job. The heart and the lungs are organs.

protect (pruh-TEHKT) to guard against harm or danger.

species (SPEE-sheez) living things that are very much alike.

thorax the middle part of an insect's body.

Web Sites

To learn more about bees, visit ABDO Publishing Company online. Web sites about bees are featured on our Book Links page. These links are routinely monitored and updated to provide the most current information available.

www.abdopublishing.com

Index